Poff the Cat

Poff the Cat

OR

When We Care

by Hartmut von Hentig

Translated by Joel Agee

Fjord Press

SAN FRANCISCO

1983

Title of German edition: *Paff, der Kater, oder Wenn wir lieben*
Published by Carl Hanser Verlag, München
Copyright © 1978 Carl Hanser Verlag München Wien

Published and distributed by:
Fjord Press
P.O. Box 615
Corte Madera, California 94925

Editor: Susan Doran
Cover design & illustration: Janet Wood
Book design & typography: Accent & Alphabet

Library of Congress Catalog Card No.: 83-82754
ISBN: 0-940242-09-5 (cloth)
ISBN: 0-940242-10-9 (paper)

Printed in the United States of America
First edition, December 1983
9 8 7 6 5 4 3 2 1

to my sister Helga

Poff the Cat

This is the story of Poff. Poff is a cat, and I have given him my solemn pledge to write this story. I don't know whether Poff cares one way or the other, wherever he is — cushioning his soul on a soft cloud somewhere in cat heaven, I guess, and letting his long, scraggly tail — I'm sure it's still scraggly — swing slowly back and forth. It's my love that's urging me to keep the promise, the love I received from Poff and have preserved for him and which, like all love, has made me richer and wiser: it demands, it exacts this avowal. An unavowed love is like stolen property, like a piece of land you've staked out somewhere high in the lonely mountains, calling it your own when actually it doesn't

9

really belong to you until the others know about it.

I confess: I did not like cats before Poff was put into my care. That has its reasons. We don't discover our deepest feelings until we have passed beyond the bounds of duty and self-abnegation. And in the beginning Poff represented a duty, no more and no less; and by that I mean something difficult, no matter what the moralists have to say about it. Poff, the approximately year-old tomcat, a tenant of the house whose basement was my domain, companion to my little friend Dody, was "handed over" to me along with the rest of the building's inventory when Dody and his parents went to Europe for a year.

The taxi stood with its motor humming in front of the door, much too early, packed full of luggage and last-minute additions, the perfect embodiment of melancholy departure; the neighbors had gathered on their porch to watch. We said "goodbye" and "have a good trip" for the seventh time; a fine drizzle began to come down; no effects were spared, every touch and nuance contributed to making the moment of leavetaking as distressing, no, as wrenchingly painful as possible. Only Poff took it all in with his characteristic nonchalance, something I had never noticed in him until then. Dody had picked him up, wrapped his small right arm around Poff's belly and was running back and forth, trying to match the conveyance of his few treasures to the adults' mood of important agitation. And there was Poff, dangling from Dody's arm with his legs stretched stiff and a look of mournful acquiescence in his eyes, a look which I noticed with an uneasy conscience, since it was not really meant for anyone to see. Then Dody was called, he hurried to the car, kissed Poff square on the nose, put him down, and climbed in. The door was slammed. Poff looked up once more, as if to take final cognizance, and then, with his neck outstretched, walked off down the street with measured steps.

Farewells are a foolish human invention; we make an awful fuss about them and forget that every moment is a farewell. Poff made me ashamed of myself, for after having given that moment no more than its due significance, he bore the pain of separation for weeks, coming back, as if purposely, to the habits that had come to an end on that day. I, on the other hand, remained standing at the curb, grinning and waving after my friends until the car finally turned the corner, and in this way I tasted the ceremony of human folly to the dregs.

There was work waiting for me in my basement room (a more comfortable place than the name suggests)—books, writing assignments, an unmade bed. I was a student, writing my dissertation and living the peculiar life of a scholar, surrounded by the greatest minds of the centuries, but alone nonetheless. I was working on Thucydides and had a sense of being engrossed in a serious, extremely incisive, ongoing conversation. I didn't notice until later that I was actually talking to myself. It's always that way: our solitude is deepest when we disguise it with the noise we make for our own distraction.

Suddenly I thought of Poff. He had eaten his breakfast and gone for a walk. I knew he wouldn't come right back, as we people often do when we've forgotten something or changed our mind. Nevertheless I stood up and opened the basement door leading to the back yard— the "drawbridge," as an old friend of mine called it, because it was locked with such a complicated system of bolts and chains and because it made a truly medieval racket when opened.

The spring sun was shining on the small untended lawn, and I soon forgot that I'd interrupted my work for the sake of Poff. I gathered together my books and moved out into the yard. It was around noon when Poff was suddenly sitting by the fence, looking at me. I paid him no further notice, but near the end of a difficult sentence I glanced up in order to think, and my eyes inadvertently fell on the cat again. He was still facing me, his position unchanged. The sentence got mixed up, I had to start it from the beginning, made a little progress, pondered, and in the midst of it became aware that again I was looking at Poff—a rather ordinary cat, and not mine either.

I noticed how beautiful and masculine he looked—yet without the toughness of a grown animal. He was gray, dark, indistinctly striped, a regular alley cat with a thick muff that framed his chin from ear to ear and gave him the appearance, when he sat up, of having a mighty barrel chest.

I called out his name in a questioning tone: "Poff?" The word stirred all the solitude around me. Poff sat motionless, but with a lurking tautness. My call was swallowed up in his impassivity. I stood up courageously, and simultaneously he rose to his feet. When I approached him to a yard's distance, he turned about-face and ran along ahead of me, as if to show me the way, and stopped in a stance of eager expectancy at the front door, his hind legs drawn tightly together, his chin, neck, and front legs a single vertical line. Sorry, buddy, this door's locked now. I picked him up and carried him to the back door, set him down again, and went up to the kitchen to get him something from the refrigerator. Poff meanwhile danced around me, rubbing my legs, first with his tail, then with his back, and finally, emphatically, with his head. Then suddenly he stepped back, casting off all affection, and looked up at me with a cool and demanding gaze. He ran to the corner where his bowl usually stood, and waited. In the meantime I'd found something suitable among the victuals my friends had left behind—a half-open, half-empty can of sardines. I scraped what was left onto a saucer and set off in the direction of the

basement, a little too proud of my pedagogic intention of getting him accustomed
to his new living quarters. Poff came after
me as if to put a halt to my error, watched
incredulously from above as I walked
down the stairs, and then, comprehend-
ing, and not at all ruffled, followed me
down in three bounds. I put the saucer on
the floor. Poff looked on with interest but
with no sign of greed. Only after I had
given him an encouraging nod did he get
down to business, performing it with
dignity.

That is exactly how each of our feeding
times proceeded, every morning and evening for nearly a year. He never gave up
his claim to having his meals served
upstairs. Never did he bear me a grudge
for my stubbornness, nor did he ever re-
spond with anything but good sense and
straightforwardness and perfect decency.

He repudiated all attempts at training. When, a little while later, I had used up the food reserves and switched to the canned dog food that had been prescribed for him (adding some appetizingly fishy-smelling cat food), he took umbrage at what he perceived as a needlessly slow procedure and returned to his corner, settled down fussily, and waited there, keeping an inner and outer distance, till I would come to the end of my preparations. This is not to say that Poff was unreceptive to ritual. We had a sacred agreement, for instance, that he would not attack the food until I had given him permission. Such rituals must have been of his own devising, and were, I still suspect, intended to educate me. Nothing is quite as embarrassing as to have held someone in lower esteem than he has held us and to be shown up by him for that very reason. So I was annoyed at first; I let the animal run off and hastily returned to my work.

I couldn't get Poff out of my mind that day, no matter how hard I tried. I convinced myself I ought to watch him closely so I could tell my friend Dody about him — as if I needed a pressing reason to notice Poff at all! I told myself I'd have to check to see whether I'd closed the door to the kitchen. I imagined I could hear him meowing or scratching somewhere. But those were very common sounds in my neighborhood, and even if it *were* Poff, why should that bother me?

In the evening I locked up the house, called Poff, and was almost pleased to find him gone: serves him right, the arrogant creature. Let him figure out for himself where he'll spend the night.

I was accustomed to reading until close to midnight. My desk stood by the basement window, which began near ground level, reaching from about the height of my chest to the edge of the low ceiling. It was one of the first warm days of the year, so I could afford to leave the window open while I sat there. Once in a while the wind would stir up a dried leaf and drive it against the grating in front of my window... I thought it was Poff. Several yards away two cats cried mournfully with human voices. The moon rose; someone was endeavoring to park a car in the narrow lane. I kept reading for a long time, without understanding much of what I read. Poff didn't come home that night.

Every morning at six I'd go out running on a park-side street in the neighborhood. As I left the house and ran past the front entrance, I saw Poff sitting in front of the door, huddled up tight, blinking, freezing. He rose up just a very little bit, and I, forgetting myself for a moment, gave him a friendly greeting. Then, thank God, I had to keep running. I ran faster and with less effort than usual, because I wasn't thinking of running. As I returned to our block, I could see Poff in the distance. I armored myself with an air of practicality, sternly called the cat's name in passing, and expected him to follow me to the back entrance. I left the door open behind me, turned on the radio for the news, put a pot of water on the stove for coffee, and stepped under the shower, performing my habitual routine with accentuated efficiency. All the while I was well aware that

Poff hadn't followed me. Inwardly I scolded him for his defiance — and at the same time I gloried in it, for now he no longer seemed so superior, so imperturbable, so self-sufficient.

His defiance was the first distinct response I'd gotten from him, a reply directed to me and my actions alone, a stone cast into the pit of solitude. And suddenly — while the water ran through my hair, down my face and over my closed eyes, and my thoughts streamed through me uninterrupted like a physical current, without my conscious direction — I realized I had been hurt, that something had penetrated my innermost bastion, my loneliness. It wasn't the fact that we were a twosome of sorts, he and I; it was that I saw his freedom, and that it hurt me. None of this came as a complete surprise; I recognized my condition with the satisfaction of one who falls ill and suddenly realizes it's an old and long-accustomed malady.

Today I can smile at the fact that it was just a cat that challenged me in my solitude. But I know that never did a more severe trial and transformation take place than in my love for this animal. Animals aren't taken in by disguises. Everything has its inescapable consequence, everything has to be immediately earned: there are no concessions, indulgences, reconciliations—all there is is justice. It's a primitive code compared to the refined contracts that obtain between human beings, but it is also clearer, more honest, more humble. In our dealings with animals we bear all the consequences of our actions alone; our rashness, our injustice, falls back upon us. The animal goes undeterred and innocent on his way, leaving us with the shame of our own failing.

I turned off the shower and saw Poff finally ambling into the house, yawning the stiffness out of his limbs, completely oblivious of me. He suddenly stopped in his tracks at the sight of a trickle of water that came inching across the dusty floor toward the drain. Every kind of motion attracted Poff's attention, and in this as much as in his dealings with people I always saw him as an artist. He ducked down before the animated creature of his imagination, eluded its reach, caught up with it, teased it along with little taps, retarded it with a hooked paw, and imparted to the water such a quivering, individualized semblance of life that I, too, was fascinated. I was reminded of a game I had discovered when I'd had to spend several weeks in prison. The windows of our cell were way up near the edge of the very high ceiling; the thick wall slanted down from the bottom of the windows to the floor. Whenever it rained, single drops would run down this incline, haltingly at first, along crooked byways, and then in a straight headlong rush. My cellmate and I would set up races between these drops and place bets on them.

Poff suddenly turned away from his plaything and looked at me with keen attention. It was as if a person were watching me as I toweled myself off, and I felt uncomfortably self-conscious — even though Poff was, of course, a "man." He seemed to be considering the meaning of the situation for a moment. Apparently he found my behavior sufficiently plausible for him to set aside his own wishes for the time being: his next move was to search for a suitable place to take a brief morning nap. When I sat down on the edge of my bed to eat breakfast, he came to join me, purring, lay down beside me, and stayed there as if to remind me of his own needs. I had completely forgotten the unresolved issue of the night he'd spent outside and his tardy response to my call in the morning.

Poff could at any time persuade you that disputes over things past are senseless, and that pedagogy is valuable, indeed possible, only in exact proportion to the pupil's willingness at the moment. I have never experienced a more complete pedagogic disaster, or one that I was more painfully ashamed of, than on that same day, when I took it upon myself to housebreak Poff, aiming at immediate effectiveness that would reach backward and forward in time. I had set up a sandbox, actually an old rectangular roasting pan filled with some rather dirty soil from the unused flower boxes on the balcony. On that day,

Poff didn't use the box, but the basement reeked. I conducted a thorough search and finally found the corpus delictum in the furthermost corner beneath the stairs — a place that could only be reached with a great deal of effort. If only he had done it in the middle of the room! I was unwilling to admit that it was pure and innocent decency that had driven him — literally — "into a corner." Getting rid of the mess took a lot of time, a lot of will power, and many a heartfelt curse. When Poff came home, I unleashed a thunderstorm to which he failed to display anything like the cowering response I'd intended. Thereupon I deliberately rekindled my rage, seized him by the collar, carried him to the place of his misdeed (the scent still lingered) and then to the sandbox, pressed his nose a little too deeply into the sand, and dropped his indignantly twisting body

27

to the ground. He scampered off, let out a few angry sneezes, and left the premises. The same mishap occurred the next day, but he had also used the box. Patiently and with a certain relief, I cleaned up and then gathered together some boards and nails and blocked off that corner, which was so hard to get to and spoke so plainly of Poff's discretion and my stupidity.

I began a new life, a fuller and more understanding kind of life, for it was no longer just my own. I had to make allowances, and for these concessions I was repaid with an increasing normality in our relations. We coordinated our habits; a different sort of "rightness" took the place of the one I was accustomed to; I began to understand that there is a special joy to be found where rules and regulations recede into the background. Joy is the fulfillment of justified desire; our more arbitrary wishes are better enjoyed in fantasy than in fulfillment, which always brings consequences in its wake. The greatest enemy of pleasure isn't its opposite, pain, but fear and a damaged conscience.

I learned that male cats have to be outside at night and that they only use a catbox once; and Poff, for his part, accepted the back door — without, however, giving up his morning wait by the front entrance. On long evenings he would come sneaking into my room and jump into my lap at an appropriate moment, warming himself and me, creating by his whole manner such an intimate feeling of mutually sheltering warmth that it made up for any inconvenience. And actually there was no inconvenience. Poff's movements, his attempts and temptations, were so supple,

so graceful and skilled, that I gladly shared
my work time with him.

How little people know about cats, I
thought, and how telling is their love for
dogs. They want slaves, selfless servants,
creatures of their own sentiment. In the
case of cats, too, all they really care for is
their own misapprehension. You hear
them saying things such as: cats only love
themselves; they flatter and rub up against
you but all they're really out for is themselves; all you get from petting them is dirt
on your hand.

But that isn't the true and complete explanation. When Poff got up from my lap
and climbed onto the desk and stalked
about among my books and papers in
order finally to leap onto the windowsill
and stare out into the cold night — without
ever overturning or soiling or displacing
anything — all this was still completely

part of that comfort and closeness that he had sought on my lap. But he didn't do it out of self-love; to my mind, he did it "in freedom." Thus Poff taught me to recognize the precarious relationship between freedom and love and to discover a greater kind of friendship, uncontaminated by those narrow distinctions of "selfless" and "self-serving" love.

I had apparently been living in deliberate isolation. I had loved, but without courage. I had made rules for my love and I guarded it with the strictest vigilance. My love had to be pure and selfless. The much admired phrase of Philine in Goethe's *Wilhelm Meister* — "And what if I love you, is that your concern?" — had found my zealous contempt. The very suggestion that I loved in this fashion would have been enough to make me hate. It would

31

have seemed to me the most contemptible of all temptations; such freedom would have meant the end of my love, which I considered to be a greater thing than any kind of freedom. My love aspired to slavery; this slavery was not self-serving; it was the perfection of love. I still fear Philine's words, but only because it is so difficult to accept the distance and indifference of the beloved. Today I am wary of intricate self-deception, of false resignation; back then, I hated freedom.

It was Poff who taught me that it doesn't matter how one loves, so long as one loves at all. Whoever says Poff's love can't be compared with a human being's is right, no doubt. Nevertheless Poff revealed to me the miracle of innocent creaturely love and moved me to accept and affirm it. Poff had an unwavering and constant faith in his love. He bore his pain no more easily than I did but with greater confidence, and what we call a cat's "instinct," in derogatory distinction from our conscious feelings, had about it both the holiness and the martyrdom of the unconscious. The slightest gesture of affectionate understanding on my part triggered torments of conjecture. Poff was even further from redemption than I was, and for this reason his superiority was both humbling and instructive. Above all: his love was unrestricted. It was an element unbounded by any form, without direction or center.

Poff generally slept on the bare wooden floor next to my bed, even though there were several old armchairs that would have given him greater warmth and comfort.

Sometimes he would get up at night and reach out with his paw in the direction of my face, as if to see whether I was still there. Around three o'clock he would clamber onto my desk and gaze out the window, which in the fall was partially blocked by dirty leaves and in winter by snowdrifts that often left only a small strip free at the top. There he would stand for a while and tell me his wishes with body language. I've already said this: Poff was an artist. He understood a lot about the expressive power of gestures. Perhaps he was collecting himself for his adventure or trying to come to terms with it, since it was not only tempting but dangerous and necessary as well. Then he would look back at me in the dark room. I would usually be awake by then. My friendship and Poff's expectation were stronger than the demands of the body. If, however, my work had kept me at my desk until late, those first hours of slumber might be more profound than usual, and I would stay asleep; then Poff would utter one brief complaint with an almost inaudible voice — pleading forgiveness, at the same time, for his lack of faith — and we would both leap into motion, he off the desk and I out of bed. By the time I had reached the door, he'd already be standing there on his hind feet, leaning against the doorjamb, pawing the bolt with impatient expectancy. I would remove the chain-lock, pull the iron bar out of its fastenings with a clang, and "let down the drawbridge."

The night is cool, and the starry sky seems clear, and yet a fine, even mist has obliterated the many small stars, so that only the large and venerable constellations remain. Poff, who was so impatient just a moment ago, steps out very, very slowly and, as he walks, he leisurely traces the curve of his path with his tail. He strides onto the stage of his life in the contained play of his strength. I stand there, watching him leave, until I begin to feel cold and "pull up the drawbridge." Half asleep, later on, I can hear the terrible screams of the fight, the laments of love, the female's shrieks of pain. When Poff comes home victorious in the morning, he's neither proud nor moved. What he did was done and gone in a moment, and beyond it no torment pursues him, no conscience.

"Your love, isn't it cruel, vain, and selfish, Poff?"

"No, there's no such thing: a love that is more or less unselfish. Water can't be more or less wet. Whatever I do in love, I take from myself, after all. I do it in spite of myself, I do it in self-annihilation and self-contempt. It hurts and never stops hurting, and yet it all comes back to me and gives me life and hope. Your longing for perfection is your worst selfishness. That I obey my love completely, without regret or doubt, is my humility. What makes your love so selfish and laughable is your constant wish to improve it, your endless thinking about it. All you have to know is whether you really care. The rest happens by itself."

Poff came purring to my breakfast table, enjoyed what I shared with him, and left me in peace. I don't think I ever felt jealous, because his affection was completely mine as soon as he joined me at the breakfast table. However mistrustful I sometimes felt of what seemed to be a flattering manner, I always took deep pleasure in the glow of his closeness, in the calming intensity of his presence.

All the doubt that usually makes up the torment and bliss of a loving relationship (for love is sweetest when one doesn't believe, doesn't have to believe) was absent from our life together, nor was there any impatience in it. Such sentiments would have been absurd, in any case, faced with Poff's commanding silence. And yet I know there was a true love between us, no matter how impossible that may seem to others: a love without question and without trust, without disturbance and without pain. Can't we love without trusting, as we can surely trust without loving? What is trust other than the firm belief that the other will remain faithful to himself and hence to that which I love? How profound was the lesson I learned

from my friendship with Poff—precisely
because he was only a cat, with gray,
shaggy fur, with an honest appetite, an
unimpeachable directness of feeling, a
heedlessly demanding presence that ban-
ished all loneliness. Love: the expression
of our real conciliation with ourselves. Its
measure: the time we have for the other,
abandoning ourselves because we are no
longer involved with ourselves. We fail so
often because we can take refuge in words;
we present ourselves the way we want to
be and are not; we quarrel with ourselves
and others. That cat never quarreled. By
loving me as I was, he taught me to become what I should be for him. And I
loved him with all his selfishness, because
it was part of him; no, more than that: part
of his love. With Poff, I never had to feel
ashamed of my imperfection; but in all my

imperfection, I loved him with all my might: that was his remedy for selfishness.

That I loved Poff like a real human friend, that I needed him as much as he needed me, I was to learn one day, about three months before my friends and hosts returned from Europe.

It was a winter morning when I opened the back door to begin my morning run and heard next to me a plaintive, timorous cry, the voice of a victim who cannot and does not want to conceal his defeat. When I turned around I saw a Poff who was no longer Poff: he was completely disheveled; large pieces of fur were torn out of him, leaving patches of white naked skin scored with scratch-marks. His paws were smeared with motor oil, the tail curled around them was almost completely stripped of its fur and caked with blood;

from a face dulled by shock and covered with dust he looked up at me with an infinitely pitiful gaze. And yet these weren't the worst changes: what made Poff seem so strange and made me suddenly sick at heart, was his body's expression of total abjection, a silent plea to be recognized in his misery and lifted out of his terror and humiliation into my protection and into my love. I bent down, discharging some of my agitation in activity. When I touched him, a quiver of pain and relief went through him. He tried to rise into my embrace, but couldn't. I carried him into the house to my bed, which was still warm, its blankets bunched up; I talked with urgent words that meant consolation, concern, respect, helplessness. And with the same abandonment with which he gave all of himself to his love, he now lost himself in his pain.

When I later washed his wounds with lukewarm water, he lay stretched out on the dresser as if to receive a known and accustomed kindness, and yet he must have suffered a lot under my unskilled daubing. His injuries were severe and led me again and again to imagine the fight, a whirling knot of cats, a large, fully-grown opponent who finally drives Poff into a corner and demolishes him, a hissing darkness, a desperate, utterly defeated, final burst of mortal resistance. Then the mad flight, the shivering miracle of escape, the waiting in defenseless terror, the flaring-up and quick extinction of shame when the drawbridge starts clattering . . .

Poff stayed inside during the following days. He lay still and never left the bed I had made for him next to mine out of an old saddle blanket. Twice a day I would put him outside the door, and only after he had made sure that I would wait there, ready to protect him, would he limp away into the nearest bushes.

He ate little and with suffering eagerness drank the warm milk I prepared for him. By the third day the wounds had begun to fester, and I became fearful. I would not have been able to afford a veterinarian. I searched the medicine cabinet upstairs, stirred sulfonamide into Poff's cat food, cleaned his pus-encrusted wounds with peroxide, dressed them with zinc salve, and did my best to bandage them with gauze. I had never learned about these things, and there wasn't anyone around whom I might have asked for advice. Much as I tried, at the time, to do the right thing, today I'm sure it didn't matter whether the means I used (in vague remembrance of treatments I had received for wounds) were appropriate for a cat. What he needed, more than the right salve, was my patience and understanding, the knowledge that I was actively helping him.

During that time I wrote long chapters of my dissertation, for now the exigencies of my life had converged on one point, my vagrant desires had found a goal, the unfulfilled need that prodded my thoughts and senses no longer existed.

How inescapably selfish love is, precisely in its deepest self-denial, in sacrifice and loyal service. And yet I loved Poff more in his pride than in his helplessness, more in his liberty than in surrender, more in himself than in my possession, in the secure grasp of my love. Was it not his independent will, his way of ignoring and passing me by, wasn't it his encroachment upon

my feelings and his rebuff of my isolation
that bound me to him so tightly?

This thought came to me later and is at
once true and untrue, clever and humble,
dialectical and unassuming and simple. At
any rate, I didn't realize until later that I
wanted to be hurt; that I preferred being
hurt and mocked to being forgotten.
When Poff was sick, all he wanted was
patience. I cannot give patience without
love—and I constantly poured out my
love before him, day and night. When he
no longer needed patience, I noticed he
didn't want love either, and then I could
no longer give him patience. Only love
could have taught me how and to what
purpose. It isn't true that love always and
only desires its object to be perfect; love is
never so blind as not to recognize imperfection; nor does imperfection offend love,
but rather, love prides itself on its power

to cherish what is imperfect — indeed to sustain it! The end of love is not only the end of an illusion, but of a reality.

When Poff had regained his health, he resumed his nightly excursions. At first he'd only stay out for an hour and then meow at the door, begging to be let back in. One night I was roused from sleep by terrible screams in the yard. I ran out into the snow in my pajamas and chased the fighting animals away. I don't know whether Poff was one of them. He didn't come back the next morning.

After he had been gone for two months, I sat down and wrote Dody a long letter in stiff capitals. It gave me little comfort to know that someone else would be sharing my grief. The pangs of my conscience, the absurdity of my hopes, the mistrust with which my abandonment turned against the memory of my love—no one could share that.

During those months my thoughts took strange paths, and I did strange things. There were thousands of gray cats in Chicago. I searched for Poff in every street and alley, in shops, on fire-escapes, in front yards, parking lots, window niches, everywhere, but especially in fantasy, which reaches ahead of all time and does not skip over anything in the past. My love held him shackled in imagination, and he was tearing loose: one of the two had to give, love or the image I had forged of him. What right do we have to violate reality with our vision, to load it down like a beast of burden with our failed ideals? I turned my back on reality for leaving me in the dark. I didn't want to believe in an accident or in any of the countless other possible explanations. I wasn't looking for an explanation. Poff had left me. That was all.

When I walked out of the house, I saw the empty place under the mailbox next to the door, where he usually waited; when I came home, my glance would fall on a battery of cat-food cans I had bought for him; when I went to visit the neighbors, I saw his tirelessly litter-bearing and suckling mother with her narrow head and grave care-worn eyes, a cat that seemed to have descended from the Egyptian deities; and at three o'clock in the morning I woke up to the sound of fighting cats in the lane, ran and opened the door and saw the vast starry sky, such an unexpected and therefore overwhelmingly beautiful sight in the city. I closed the door again, and the cold night air was like an enemy following me into the room. I crept back into my bed in the dark, quiet basement room and knew that it wasn't a home any longer; I no longer liked my own world.

When we love, when we care in full earnest, the world takes on an enchanted depth, and we find consolation and meaning shining from the most insignificant, simple things. When we no longer have anything to care for, when we become indifferent, when expectation has burned out, when after being hurt we first lose ourselves in our pain and eventually lose the pain itself, we find that the things we lived with and adorned ourselves with when we were happy have now lost their peace and their magic. When that happens we should leave for another place and not return—unless we've found another love, turned the soil of another

49

garden, caught fire at another promise. If we return without loving, but knowing that we should be loving, knowing that we are responsible for the terrible desolation around us, it might happen that we ourselves inflict the final blow to our last languishing kindly illusion, a memory we had left behind that was still alive with hope.

The weeks that followed were of a gray normality: proofreading the final revisions of my dissertation, preparing for the exams, moving into another apartment— a life, in short, that was heavily burdened with practical concerns and had little room left over for the pathos of a curious relationship with a cat. The notion of a neurosis, such as might befall one at the end of a period of study that required the most extreme mental and spiritual effort, did not

OR WHEN WE CARE

arise until many years later, when it occurred to me to write all this down. I never
believed in this interpretation—but that
doesn't make it less likely, of course. As it
happened, the story had a sober, unlit-
erary end.

When Poff returned after another three
months, he didn't pretend to be selfless;
cats don't know how to do that; people
think they owe themselves and each other
at least the pretense of self-denial, and in
doing so they commit the truly loveless
act.

I was no longer living in the house when
he came back. My friends had only re-
cently returned, and Poff was welcomed
by Dody as if he had just left. Poff went
back to using the front entrance, lay on
the sofa upstairs, let himself be warmed

by the sun and petted by Dody and his parents. His scars scarcely aroused any surprise, the memory of his deeds and his suffering was swallowed up by his mute, matter-of-fact presence. On the day when I came to visit him, he paid me no notice at all. His masters told me he'd developed an Oedipus complex, that he was pursuing his mother and delivering nightly serenades in the garden next door. I felt sad and rejected. After another week, Poff disappeared forever. His successors were compared to Poff by Dody and found wanting, and he may even have mistreated them outright.

There was a bookstore on 55th Street. On top of the remaindered and marked-down books that were displayed on a special table lay a cat which at first I mistook for

Poff. I dashed into the store and hurried to the table. The tomcat that blinked at me there was a stranger. He lifted his undamaged, bushy tail a little, as if in deliberate remonstrance, closed his eyes and went back to sleep. In disbelief I searched through his fur for scars, but there were none. I stood staring into space, as if robbed. "Are you looking for anything in particular?" the salesman asked. "That one over there!" I said, with my hand still hovering over the cat's tail. The man pushed the cat aside a bit and picked up a book. "Do you mean this one?" On the dust jacket it said: Sherwood Anderson, *When We Care*. I said, "Yes."